The Object of the Subject.

The Philosophical Hack:
The Second Part

II

For my daughter,
Marley Joy Prusmack,
       the original *thiccbeefcake69*.

Who didn't give two shits about philosophy.

May she rest in power and peace.

       May 2019

IV

The Philosophical Hack:
The Second Part.

The Object of the Subject

By Cedric Nathaniel

O D D   P A R C E L   2 0 1 9

V

The Object of the Subject. The Philosophical Hack:
The Second Part

First Printing: September 2019 (2)

ISBN 978-0-359-76250-7

OD PARCEL
Louisville. Colorado.

secondmusic.org

The Philosophical Hack:
The Object of the Subject

The Second Part

"What the hell are you talking about?"

Every philosophical enterprise concerning truth should begin with the question *"what the hell you are talking about?"*. If the questioning begins with any other question, then we know we are involved with a conventional effort and that the purpose is to uncover something more or less real.[1] If we begin with meaning, then we can mark the position of the subject; if it is about what is as stake, then we know there is an ethical concern about actions, outcomes and such. Without the question, "what the hell are you talking about?" we begin at an intact philosophical position (the *True Object*) and develop or fill out the ramifications of that identity.

---

[1] This is the basis of the *ontological argument*, what we could call the *ontological method* or the *conventional philosophical method*. The ontological method, for a term, is a particular method which positions the subject in reality. Conventional philosophy concerns ontological arguments.

We found in The First Part that when we speak of truth we must speak in a certain manner. Hence, we call the philosophical investigation into aspects of reality a *conventional* philosophical question based in ontological certainty. With reference to this certainty, the phenomenon of the central thinker is already understood, and we move onward to find our seats at the ideological table. With reference to the Event,[2] ideology is religious and involved with a scholastic type for discussing cosmology and ethics.[3] When we ask "what the hell are you talking about", we have displaced cosmological givens, ceased with offending accusations and their correlational defensive assumptions, and show our intention as being fully invested in having *no* position at the table.

---

[2] The difference between the Event and an event is part of the meaning of this essay.

[3] I associate the conventional philosophical method with Scholasticism because it is a method of learning which relies heavily upon institutional normative knowledge and functions to include or otherwise absorb every possibility of plurality through ideological exclusivity; i.e. the Postmodern condition.

4

In this manner of speaking, the concern of the negotiation table is always, by definition, the transcendental progress of higher forms of Being. The negotiation involves agents of transcendence getting something done, and given the nature of the common human sort, we must be not only versed, but skilled in strategy and tactics and assume until proven otherwise that we are involved in playing a game of poker. We must be this figure of the mistaken kind of Socratic irony, learn to play the game of deception that we might be keen upon when and where to open. In general, though, the main thing to learn at the table is to never show your cards, to recognize that the game never ends and that the ledger is never to be balanced; one has to be right with these parameters to play. Progress is the ever-growing pot, while fulfillment and emancipation occur when everyone is all in or have all checked. Unfortunately, this never occurs because no one is ever all in—that is part of the deception inherent to the ideological game—and no one folds.

*

5

Watching the game, and never quite knowing who is waiting for a seat at the table, the philosopher asks a fellow onlooker whether she is in or out. Her answer reveals her intension[4] and whether she found a seat. No one ever leaves the game nor sits out a hand; anyone who leaves the table is a *check,* which is a type of bluff.

"What the hell are you talking about?" she asks.

*

A *bluff* is a tactical embankment, a high ground from which one can see the layout of the land. The bluff is not a political move because the good bluff is that by which no *tell* is revealed; politics is about always having a tell and being able to find it in another through the negotiation or interaction. The successful bluff takes not only the hand but the whole game because the variations in presentation are understood by the other people at the table as indications of what is dishonest and what

---

[4] As noted in The First Part, the spelling *intension* emphasizes what is 'in' tension in one's intention.

is honest, the assumption being that there is an honesty that can be discerned amongst the general play of dishonest motions, the *tell,* moves that are based in a strategic agenda. In this way the other players are always showing *their* tell. By playing exactly by what the rules of the game would dictate except in that foundational area of being honest or dishonest, the bluff, as a continuing tactic, is a manner of staying always hidden: The honesty is that the move is totally and always dishonest with respect to the other players' understanding of things, but not to the rules of the game. In other words, there is no strategy.

Deontology

Exception is the meaning of deontology. The rules of the game here are that a person must be honest and dishonest as varying times and conditions. What is deontological with respect to these rules is that to follow the rules one must be *entirely* honest; this is to say that those who play by the rules of contingency are in fact behaving ontologically. In a similar vein as Emmanuel Kant and his analogies from discourse,[5] deontology is often misunderstood as a

---

[5] The various types of knowledge and judgments made upon them is the topic of Emmanuel Kant's *Critique of Pure Reason*. Many philosophers understand his discussions to be about what can be found out through analyzing various propositions and that an analysis of propositions through his manner is supposed to yield a way to make proper choices, that is, judgments. I suggest that he uses the *analogy* of the structure of propositions to make his point, and that applying his method to various propositions yields very little philosophical significance, even while answers derived in that way may yield conventional uses.

strategy by which to make choices. Ontological choices are said to be made due to natural impulses, such as goodness, innate to being human; ethical choice based upon group or individual survival or evolutionary adaptation of behavior are also ontologically based. A true reading of deontology, though, despite the extended, involved high definition and theoretical extrapolations, can be said to have more to do with logistics than natural impulses. Here, rules, and not natural inclinations, dictate what is *allowed* to be done, how activities are able to be accomplished and still count as legitimate, and this includes how one speaks or uses discourse. In fact, deontology is entirely discursive in a very Kierkegaardian way.

It is Soren Kierkegaard who shows us the ethical universe is a categorical imperative of knowledge; he writes "the universe is the ethical"[6] and moves through

---

[6] Soren Kierkegaard, *Fear and Trembling*. Also; we get the *categorical imperative* from Kant. Though conventional philosophy enjoys keeping choice as part of the game (what they hell are they talking about?), a more precise definition is a category which

his works to describe the possibility of an existence which does not accord with ethics, but indeed is nevertheless *entirely ethical,* as opposed to the common manner of ethics which understands the partiality of being human in the universe. The point to understand is that what is entirely ethical is so by virtue of its only choice arriving between behaving in the 'ethical-universal' (we could say *real*) manner and behaving in a manner that for all reasonable purposes is absurd, which is to say, by definition, *not* ethical, or, not a part of the universal mode.[7]

---

occurs consistent with its Being: A category that cannot occur except in accordance with the category of itself.

[7] Note that the issue of this essay concerns an orientation upon objects (see The First Part); as Lance Kair has said, in this new consideration of things, we turn the notion of *faith* on its head. So likewise, the reader will wish to understand the relationship between Kierkegaard's "universal/ethical" category with what this essay's use of the "universal object", or what we shall also call the "True Object".

Kierkegaard makes the point about what it is to be a subject; he thus marks out how the *ethical* world is indeed the *universal* world, but that the subject need not be confined by the dictates of this ethical

If we can understand ethics as a generally unwritten but noticed compendium of rules by which things attain as well as then retain what is 'correct-right-good-sane' and 'incorrect-wrong-evil-insane',

---

universe. He thus suggests that the subject determined in its state thus has already made the move which is absurd by ethical standards, which is to say, already does not need to reckon the essence or totality that is itself in a universe where a choice to be free is not understood in its inherent contradiction. He calls this determined state *faith*, such that all one has to do in life is make the absurd choice into authenticity.

This essay as well will elaborate that where one does not come upon the absurd choice, there does the subject remain a real identity involved entirely with reality which is constituent of *True Objects*. So, in contrast to this real manner of coming upon things (objects), this essay seeks to thus find the object of the subject, or how the subject is indeed a Universal Object, all the while allowing for the metaphysical and religious ideals which finds the subject in the middle of semantic objects of its phenomenological subjective experience. This is to say, wherein and about which Kierkegaard sees the absurd (authentic) contra ethical-universal, this essay sees Universal Objects contra True Objects. The two schemes are complimentary rather than reductive.

11

then we can begin to have purchase upon the *bluff* mentioned above and how it allows for total honesty through the feat of being entirely dishonest. Deontology would have it by virtue of the totality of things that there must be a totality that is equally not of that 'things'; this is to say, that a set of partial objects would include an object that is not partial, which it then excludes categorically, i.e. actively denies. This player exits the game and no longer has a seat at the table due to the bluff, where the game is still played ethically through a deontological proxy that is usually called the *agent of transcendence*.

See that this situation does not necessarily describe an 'unethical agent',[8] or one that does whatever she wants. Rather, this agent upholds the exclusivity of the real universe through its deontological position where by the rules, as a universal class, are followed though the absurd choice, or, as Lance Kair has suggested in my previous book, a choice that cannot be made,[9] in

---

[8] There is a discussion to be had about how evil may not be merely a cultural convention.

[9] Lance Kair, *The Moment of Decisive Significance*.

contrast to a choice that is made of options through free will. This is to define the state by which one makes choices: The Two Routes.[10]

Existence is not mutually exclusive to anything else; as we will see, as a founding term it is exclusive only to existence itself. Existence is particularly *plural* with respect to the condition of the *two*. The One Route mentioned earlier is that route which understands the basis of existence as plural and the subject but one of a multitude of existent things in the single universe with definite and irrefutable laws to which all universal things answer.[11] The other route is the route in question, the absurd situation of

[10] See also The First Part. Being occurs along two mutually exclusive routes. This essay discusses the possibility of the Two Routes.

[11] The existence of multiple universes depends first upon the recognition of multiplicity in the cardinality (best) of our universe and its ordinal primacy (first); which is to say, our universe is singular by the definition implicit to the use of the term, and our universe must first exist for there to be knowledge of the possibility of multiple universes. This is to say, that we must, in the fullest sense, first come to terms with what it means to be human in the universe.

the Event, that which brings Reason into question. The juxtaposition of these two conditions grant us a view upon the Event of this essay—as a real answer and not merely a state of questioning. The issue of The Two Routes is not toward the understanding which reduces back into unity, but rather concerns a suspension which stays suspended.

*

The Event of Slovoj Zizek's book of the same name marks an ontologically duplicitous circumstance. In the history of modern philosophy at least, a specter has haunted reason. Laying low in the shadows, the part that would just sometimes be caught be the light is, or was, called *irony*. Irony is the culprit in the problems of philosophy because of the manner that philosophy has instated Reason.[12] So it should come to no surprise to us that the Event might interest

---

[12] See below for a further discussion about Kant's *Pure Reason*. Also, reason is by its nature *not unitive*, does not speak of a common sort, even as it uses reflection and grants appearance toward ideological unity.

us currently; almost too coincidental to the times, we wait for something of the shadows to be brought out into the light because what *was* brought out has the appearance of having failed. We wait eagerly because at times it appears we are caught in a repeating cycle of history, where we think we are getting somewhere but then find that a few or even ten years goes by and we are right back where we were, each philosophical party centered upon what any philosopher in question was 'really saying', yet everyone agreeing only in part, if even that. The agreement then starts to look more like an uneasy truce on the verge of a renewed violence, an agreement to imply a truth of the author while often never really understanding them. Of course, often enough we can find that every philosopher worth her salt will disagree with that statement; "of course I understand them—here's proof!" This then is the point of discussing the Event, because it seems something was missed that no one is noticing.[13] The Event reduced back into the One Route creates camps.

---

[13] Here is my proof: It is that you do not see!

*

True events, Zizek tells us, are 'miraculous' and occur seemingly out of nowhere, an occurrence that appears out of joint, that shocks us and disrupts everything.[14] Yet there is also something regular about an event that normalizes the flow of ideological lacking; indeed, Zizek seems to want to normalize events through an exceptional route, to bring into correspondence events such as the writing of a book and the Event of understanding, the event of knowing and the Event of communication, to show how though we may want to exceptionalize, say, spiritual events of conversion, events actually occur, present themselves or otherwise exist in the same manner at all times and everywhere. I suggest that by doing so with an *un-*intentional irony that lay at the heart of the contradiction of *a priori synthetical* reason, he is giving us a picture of the two sides of the Event. He is surely putting forth an argument to be taken in through its various measurements and weights, particularized

---

[14] Unless specifically noted, going forward, all citing for Zizek is from *Event*. This instance is from page 4.

in various types, examples and occasions, prescriptive in its manner of instructing the reader how to form the conception of his view. Yet, at the same time, he gives us an example of the descriptive and purely *presented* objectivity of the Event, it's 'in-itself' essence, if you will, evidence of the actual situation that rides over any argumentative opinions, attached to the argument only through coincidence.[15]

Through giving us an argument as well as its description, in that way, he shows how the Event itself inadvertently falls apart, cleaves neatly into two kinds of events, one that hides in the ironic transcendence of everyday life, and one that is open to a kind of interpretation that decries multivocality, where the site of transcendence itself cannot be missed in its immanent certitude. The significance in this ability of the object,[16] then, is evental in its

---

[15] Or, vicariously. See Graham Harman's essays and books. Particularly of interest, see *Tool Being* for a discussion about Heidegger's present-at-hand and ready-to-hand.

[16] The object of the subject. The meaning of object orientation will be filled out through this essay.

disruption of regularity. The reticence of the object shows us the determinizing aspect of reason itself, and there by its fault; changing the field by which change itself is reckoned, the authentic emancipatory Event is revealed.

The bad part about this whole thing is that it cannot come about through any sort of argument because what comes about is inherent in the presentation of the argument over its contexts and persuasions. Knowledge about the conditions necessary for or what defines such an Event is particularly impotent for bringing about the Event due to the nature of the operating paradigm for deploying reason. Knowing that an Event should occur in this way or knowing what to look for as an Event does nothing to change the field; the event thus stays a normal feature of reality whereby events can have different significances and meanings. Thus, this is not an argument disguised as a description; the description of the situation does not have an underlying motive to dismantle, deconstruct or otherwise discredit to imply or suggest that something else should be done or be another way: This is not an *ethical judgement*; it is a *description of* facts. Discussion through the presentation of argumentative contexts is *thus* not an incorrect way of getting things done; rather, the description acts more as a view into what is actually being done, what is actually occurring and not as a rebuttal to its proposed antagonist.

The evental nature of common experiences allow us to reject the circular and determined nature of belief and point toward causes and outcomes, most often in a manner to direct decision. Such events work to verify to ourselves that we had something to do with it. Zizek points out some common circular oddities that we can easily recognize in reflection which motivate us to activity. Love, for example, does not encompass the detail to culminate in loving someone, rather, it is love that makes the details of the person radiate. Similarly, there is nothing inherent to religious arguments that cause me to be a believer; it is only once I am a believer that these arguments have significance. And again; war does not develop because of protests and civil unrest, but we cannot discount how such aspects were involved with it. The appreciation of art is notoriously more than its parts. As we can

generalize an event to what is common of
human experiences, the appearance of any
event seems to surmount its causes; the
reason we explain into the event seems to
have more to do with grounding it in the
sense of reality more than it does any true or
knowable causes. So, if we can be honest
about it, we might admit that the Event
arises from an effective nowhere and that
conventional philosophy is the effort to
define what nowhere is, to then remove the
gaping hole in reason which appears with the
Event. "At first approach, an event is... the
effect that seems to exceed its causes."[17]

*

We should note, quickly, before we
get too far, that Zizek recruits the
terminology and associated concepts of
Jacques Lacan, namely the three aspects or
modes of psychoanalysis: The Real, the
Symbolic and the Imaginary. I will use these
ideas also, but I do not define the relation to
them up front because they are intimately
tied in with the Event. Their definition, how
they are used and what exactly they mean

---

[17] Zizek, p. 5

for the Event will be disclosed by the end of the essay. The reader may notice my use of the terms *real, reality,* and such, and though it could appear that I am using them under a different guise than Zizek and Lacan, I am indeed using them not dissimilarly than their usual (Lacanian) psychoanalytical meanings. This will become apparent as we proceed.

Reality is a political structure. Though we can use different tropes to scaffold meaning in different configurations, it is very difficult to escape the consequences of the identities presented by them in the political world. We can then see clearly that the Event is most often normalized to remove its exceptional status (the notice of exception is normalization[18]); whatever was indeed miraculous becomes just part of the real scene, explained in the context of other real events. Earlier we saw how reality and the

---

[18] The Event is that which traverses the real political field. The issue we treat in this essay concerns that which does not return to politics while allowing politics to do its business.

pass function together as religious faith.[19] In this way we can define a limit which locates the parameters of a real cosmology through recent philosophical 'turns', as they are called, or perhaps 'approaches', as seems more appropriate.

---

[19] That which allows thought to overcome contradictory senses of experience is called a *pass*. See The First Part.

Philosophical Approaches

The key philosophical turns or paradigms for this essay are the *modern,* and the *post-modern.*[20] If philosophy is able to be understood as a progressive process of knowledge for human understanding of ourselves and the world, then these paradigms serve to outline human knowledge through how consciousness (the psyche) operates. In short and in general, one stabilizes and one destabilizes. Together they define a closed terrain or territory,[21] and in this way constitute the current paradigm of reality; they show what the human being is by what it does, and thereby

---

[20] We can no longer rely upon discourses that arise merely out of inspiration.

[21] The First Part described briefly Gilles Deleuze and Félix Guattari's notion of *deterritorialization.* The point there is due to their presentation of what gives as it takes, we are able to thus move outside of the political reality to describe the object which is giving and taking..

allow us a view into our current situation as subjects of an intrinsic mythology, or the currently more acceptable (if not more offensive), real religion.

Paradigms occur in moments that defy any current models for prediction; by definition, predictions only involve intra-paradigm elements (hence the interest in maintaining the status quo). The paradigm which operates presently for philosophy was closed off by Martin Heidegger and his *Dasein*, or "being-there", to make a definition of region possible. Dasein can be said to be the disclosure of the Event of Being to knowledge (human Beings), which coincides with the Collapse un-coded by Ludwig Wittgenstein.[22] The two defining limits of what we shall generalize to call Modern, the 'escape routes' that define what is closed off, are noted as *Modern* and *Post-modern*.

---

[22] See The First part. The paradigm which operates now even while closed off is part of the impetus for this essay. The disclosure of Being to knowledge put to use by reason develops the irony of Being closed off that we call *alienation* in one sense, and *correlational* in another. In this move, access is regained.

Together they form the religious apology of the mythological paradigm we understand and operate within as reality.[23]

The *Modern* mode is defined by transcendence. Despite the various eras of the scholarly historian, modernity is an annoyingly persistent overlying of transcendence upon existence by reason; always there is a positing of what cannot be proven onto what is apparent and what is religious in this regard is the assumption of what should be apparent by all parties. The atheist is annoyed with the theists, and vice versa. The farmer annoyed with the trader of finance, and vice versa. The regular person is annoyed with technology; the Silicon Valley tech-star cannot understand how technology is pointless. Key-shortcuts on computers are annoying and frustrating to some while wonderfully efficient to others. History was incorrect in *this* way, and history verifies the various points we wish to make in *that* way. Everywhere and at all times modernity brings in the transcendent aspect to be concerned with itself; the Wall

---

[23] We call the functional system of this religious outline of modernity *Capitalism*.

Street wizard who relies upon her wits to make powerful business deals; the business owner who does yoga to allow him to center on what he has to do today to make and sell the best pastries; the dog walker who has to negotiate eight dogs down a busy city street and pick up after them. Transcendence brings the appearance of reality into focus by presenting us the conditions for existence, from the daily insistences and nuances of social interaction, to the great and deep physical discoveries of science, to the spiritual-magical fronts of consciousness and other planes of existence. Transcendence allows for it all to "be-there", whether it be 'only' thoughts or the 'actual' world.

Ontology or the 'ontic' is concerned with the narrow view of reality itself, "its emergence and deployment".[24] This is the *post*-modern parameter of our cosmological imperative. This is the introspective part of appearance, one could even say, the speculation upon the possibilities involved with what is given to appearance. The great scientific questions are post-/modern in orientation: Why are we here? Where are we

---

[24] Zizek, p. 6.

going? How do we fit in? Are we alone in the universe? They ask into how ontology might be deployed.

Yet we should probably not be fooled into thinking that the *post-* of modernity has moved us anywhere necessarily away from modernity; this seems to be what is commonly understood with postmodern ideals, that we are getting somewhere through understanding and using them.[25] For example, the idea of

---

[25] Postmodernity allows for the 'believing one's own script'. The only way that postmodernism is moving away from what is modern is to believe what it tells itself; namely, that reality is grounded in the postmodern method of understanding. If such a proposal were not justified by the socially ordained proponents, we would call it self-righteous privilege. Nihilism is particularly postmodern because by virtue of the self-righteousness that understands itself within a context of an ability to transcend its limitations through reasonable intension. Post-modernity is the condition of modern existence. The 'Postmodern method of understanding' is that theoretical application which outlines multitudinous modes of real difference and the potential for Being confined within the possibility of Being open. The contradiction which envelopes every permissible

nihilism is a postmodern tenant, how do we get anywhere from there? But we should also wonder how we got *here*, to nothing, because once we get to nothing we often forget that we started at *something*. The (general) postmodern conclusion of *nothing* works retroactively to bestow upon all knowledge its basis in nothing. This is so much the case that congregants of Postmodernism conveniently often forget that the theory concludes of nothing that the objects of its postmodern analysis were (or are) *modern*. It can get complicated here, but again we should not let the convoluted nature of postmodern theory guide our view without *further* analysis: The effort of such an 'analysis of nothing', what has been called "in the last instance",[26] begins to find that the wandering and often verbose explorations of subjectivity tell us not very much practical information about how to dispel the secret encodings of ideological structures and their uses for power-plays, and definitely little of how to emancipate ourselves from such

---

possibility of positive knowledge is the aspect which marks the Postmodern as a parameter of modernity.
[26] Notoriously of Francois Laruelle's Non-philosophy.

limiting ideals.[27] In the end, we find how the subjectivities show up for the ultimate purpose of maintaining the very structure of the critiquing power, and that power itself arises as the critique, or for another term, as politics.

As a social and media critique, Zizek's approach is inseparably political. We are finding that the nature of the Event might compel a subject to act in accordance to rules that are presented in the act itself, all the while withholding the subject from such a stifling reduction through the proxy. However, this has not always been the case. The phenomenological subject of time[28] occurs as a continuum of centered moments which can be pulled out of context to be viewed in various manners. These manners

---

[27] Paulo Freire's *Pedagogy of the Oppressed* tells us quite clearly how systems of oppression function: The oppressed regularly end up appropriating the ways of the oppressor to relieve their own oppression, and thereby perpetuate the oppressing systemic structure by integrating themselves functionally into the ideology instead of continuing the work of emancipation.
[28] *Phenomenology* concerns the phenomenon of Being, in particular, the *subject*.

are then found in the reduction to that center and through various discursive signals of progress, but eventually the center relents to its nothingness; hence the requirement for a proxy *now*. If there is no proxy, or agent, that can be admitted or noticed, then the contexts which relate only to themselves amount to a negotiated reality, and in fact return to establish *the* reality of relative values in negotiation as *the* true imperative of reality.[29] In a quite Jean-Paul Sartrean Existential way, the subject indeed revolts from the abyss of freedom (nothingness, contradiction, self-relation, infinite correlationalism) to then establish indemnity through the agency of discursive manipulation which finalizes in political identity. Hence *real* emancipation is defined but thereby does not arrive at the emancipatory subject of the authentic Event, for this kind of revolt is more akin to the acquiescence of denial.

*

---

[29] Ironically, this is the kind of distortion of meaning that Postmodern theory unfortunately allows for.

Zizek has not revolted (though some think he and his politics are revolting) from anything in particular. We should notice of psychoanalysis that the abyss of freedom is merely another ideological trope, a symbol which projects its object (abyss, nothingness, void) through the imaginary field of real identity. It is a matter of investment. At some point it is possible to say that an Event did manifest in such a way to present the abyss of freedom in context, which is a contradiction in terms, but the *Event* that-is-the-revolt, or the revolution-which-is-inherent, is better said to be a particular mark of Hegelian-Lacan progress.[30]

---

[30] In the case of the Event it is not proper to locate particular identities which transcend the limit of knowledge to pass into an 'actual' catalogue of idea which necessarily associate with a particular object (the issue of the founding term). This is to say that finding a True Object is not authentically evental even as it is a part of the political field of identities. Encountering text to indicate an author (e.g. Sartre, Hegel, etc...) is to show what is represented as the emancipatory subject, hence, we may come to a significance of my essay here and thus to what is evental of the situation: To wit; I am writing an expository essay about the Event that is the book by

31

Nevertheless, Zizek approaches Events in an evental way, one which, as he says, brings out the deadlocks and inconsistencies in each occasion.[31] In other words, he follows the route determined by contradiction.

---

the author Slavoj Zizek called *Event*. We will find the truncating aspect of identity with Jean-François Lyotard's work later on (i.e. the move by which nothing gains significance or justice). Nevertheless; we should not (we can and do, but what is should?) speak to what, say, Hegel means and then (seamlessly) think it means that Hegel is submitting data through the line of time (like a fiber-*ontic* cable) to arrive fully intact and uncorrupted to our minds, relying then upon our minds to properly decode the transmission. Neither Lacan. The nature of the Event is at issue here through this essay and so finds itself indicted by what I call the "Zizek-Lacan-Hegelian Platform" or what I will often abbreviate as the ZLH scheme or scaffolding. When any authors' ideas are presented in singular, it is usually implied that the truncated form is waiting to buffer from the rest of the essay having been read, and the implicit Event of such suspension.

[31] Zizek, p. 7.

Take Notice

So, where do we begin? How do we start down this road determined in contradiction?

Following the crumbs, we have been led into this essay. I have noted earlier that due to the restraints of what is allowed to be included according to the conventions of the time we must speak in a certain manner. The manner of this speaking uses Slavoj Zizek's book *Event* as a sort of map to begin to move into what is left out from the conventional philosophical view.[32]

This manner appears in reference to the path[33] like any other discourse, although it does not stick to the path. Here,

---

[32] This move does not mean the conventional method has *no* use, but only that we now have a way to find what it can be best used for.

[33] See The First Part.

we might see a language game,[34] yet unlike a conceptual structure that is used by a segregate party[35] this adventurous manner contains an inference to be verified. The invested party seeks to support a profound argument through ineffable scaffoldings that retain their integrity out of sight from the present thought, inspirations ready to be drawn out at any moment from the shadows in one instance and from the heavens in another. The inference in the operation of this essay then is that there is no hidden structure and any ontological arguments that appear in the foregoing is incidental to

---

[34] The idea of 'language games' was introduced by Wittgenstein in *Philosophical Investigations* which was published posthumously. His meaning is not inconsistent with what occurs through the Event.

[35] Reality and its conventional ontological method are upheld through an assumption of a subject sufficiently segregate from the world that it can know things about it. This is to say that in order to analyze, conceptualize or otherwise know anything about reality a subject cannot be a subject as well as the thing that is subject to analysis. The conflation (the Phenomenological reduction of knower and known) is either conceptual collapse or intensional suspension. This essay takes the route less taken of the collapse.

the case that is being presented for verification, even as ontological cases can be drawn from it.

Some eternal beings will inevitably appear, but they are not the main attraction. Though we agree that the physical manifestation of the body has most probably developed in the way anthropology and biology would describe, we are equally unsure that the usual interpretation of the overt content of the thinking brain can be used to develop an accurate representation of what consciousness *does*.

To begin his book, Zizek tells us we indeed are on a train...

And I add...along a route...[36]

We are on a train (in Zizek's book), but when we look again, it more appears like we are looking out over the passing country from a hill top, taking in views from different vantage points, or perhaps, plateaus.[37] As we ride in the train of the Event we look out the

---

[36] We have been made to retreat and regroup.
[37] See The First Part.

window, from our seat, from a different car, sometimes we go out on top of the car, like an action movie. This essay presents various views upon the countryside of the Event; here, Zizek's "stops" do not look at, then, necessary particulate types of Event as much as the stops can appear as different manners of looking at the same Event, or as perhaps Heidegger might put it, the Event of the same.

*

For this trip, we start at the end of his book where he tells us to "take special notice",[38] and we understand this in a context of return. For now, having taken in the various sites of the path, or the railroad, as the case may be, we find ourselves back at the beginning of the trip. We can start again and take special notice of what we saw before in a certain light, to see afresh the world around which the train just traveled.

The tourist stops of Zizek's train ride, in the end, are all political. We then return to take special notice because the

---

[38] *Note Bene.*

guide along the tour was telling us about the various places and different things to look at and how to look at them. Now we take special notice to see how they might –or might not – all be political in nature.

The Event

Zizek asks:

"What are the chances of an authentic political event...in which the process is the undoing of past events?"[39]

The conductor yells *All aboard!* and we start on our trip again. The Event, we hear, is a radical turning point, but one that is somehow invisible, one that is significant yet elusive. We begin to consider what an Event might be which turns our view, such that we look back, and then forward, in the attempt to find out what changed. The train is moving, and we reflect; what has changed, Zizek writes, is the very parameter by which we measure how things change. The first trip around the world showed us that change is inevitable; we heard profound aphorisms such as "the only thing that stays the same

---

[39] Zizek, p. 157.

is change". We felt comfortable in that observation and ourselves as we embraced change and attempted to conform our narrow attitudes to the vicissitudes of life and the world; yet something still continued to feel wrong. Was it all for nothing? At each contingent event, each passing scene, we continue to try to adjust our view in the attempt to gain a wider understanding of the world as it is, and to be more accepting and less judgmental. The philosopher in us thought we were getting somewhere, growing in understanding of this difficult world...

*

The philosopher sees change and measures what is real along a continuum of static knowledge, an ideal for which knowledge, as a knowable thing, is stable.[40] Events occur in a continuum of change, but

---

[40] This is not an argument about the ontological status of knowledge, rather, it is an observation of what must occur to begin to assess philosophical operations. Knowledge may at root be an ontological slurry, but we do not treat it as such in knowing it. Even the slurry is defined!

anchored, if you will, each event marking a potential to know how the world is actually constructed, how it moves, how it appears, what laws govern these aspects. She surely understands that her view is perfect in its basic ability and potential to see and know, but, often, she does not consider that such a view is likewise *sacrosanct*. The view is perfect; with the open mind and perhaps a certain empathy and consideration of the possibility of the sanctity of the world and others and their views, she understands herself within the possibility of imperfection, but this, itself, is a perfect manner of Being.[41] In fact, it can *only* be argued against; the excursive questioning it yields is perfect self, is perfect Being questioning itself against its irreproachable manner of knowing things. The philosopher notices this contradiction and yet is unable to bring about the seeming methodological necessity to consider itself outside of itself; which is to say, as an object. The view is always subjective. At every turn the answer yields to a gaping question that apparently cannot be filled. She resolves and concludes that this is the absolute condition

---

[41] Another aphorism: The only perfection is imperfection.

of being human, the limit at which no human being can go past: The Cartesian world.

She returns to her experience. She takes another trip, carrying that open mind that is ultimately limited in the concept of openness. She considers that there must be some sort of intervening aspect that disrupts the closed loop of the open mind, because indeed it feels as well as appears that the open mind is coming upon and ascertaining things of the world through an opening which does not, in any way – except though the logical consideration of it – appear closed off. Something must be wrong. She comes back home and considers the problem again.

Can you see it?

The basic problem of the philosopher of our time is the inability to have an answer which does not again bring up the same question of correlation. The problem is emancipation; it is the problem of the emancipatory subject. The question concerns how to come upon an Event which transforms the condition by which the Event itself was come upon? But an even more preposterous question arises: How can the subject know of such an event? If a possibility exists where the condition by which the subject is known can be changed, is the subject capable of knowing that such an event occurred? As we proceed around the circumscribing path again, the main issue of the Event is if we could witness such a change. Can there be an Event that is a turning point through which the past is changed and witnessed as such? If the parameters by which change is measured are indeed changed, then, the question of the political Event becomes its visibility: Can you see it?[42]

The issue we face of the political subject is not so much about conservatism. We are not here in the philosophical interest of preserving an ontological reduction to an essential or absolute freedom; we are in the parallel business of observation. If the issue was about conservatism, then we would not be having this kind of discussion. Indeed, we could not consider a change in the manner by

---

[42] The question "Can you know it?" is a different question. This essay is also addressing the relation of viewing and knowing.

which change is gauged, because the nature of change itself would be understood as unchangeable, i.e. the manner by which change is reckoned is free or contingent. This is what Zizek means when he says in capitalism things change so they can stay the same.[43] The issue arises only in the light of liberty as much as we take the notion of freedom to its end and ask if there is an *actual* freedom, which is no different than asking if liberty arises from the institution of state, or if it is indeed inalienable or essential to Being (human, at least). The conservative vote would never ask these questions because the very mention of freedom is axiomatic to any essence that might be questioned; by definition, conservative is that which *keeps* or *holds values in place*. It is only *in* the questioning that the issue arises, albeit by the 'un-held' element.

The open economy of this dichotomy is the basis of the Western democratic state, though one could never find a single representative of such ideals. The state is a dynamic situation of conservative and liberal

---

[43] Zizek, p. 159

aspects. *Politics* is the negotiation of power through exchange; in this grounding area, what is exchanged involves that which is kept in place and that which is not, or that which is 'liberated'. When we speak of politics, we speak about the 'values kept' interacting with the values that are 'not kept', or free from the bound identity. The realm or area where this exchange occurs is called the *economy*. The precise formulation of the question of the Event is whether the emancipatory change can be witnessed by everyone, or, at least by one who then represents the subsequent and perhaps more significant question: Can this Event be communicated? If there is an Event which changed the field by which change is reckoned, can this new state be communicated to the old? To wrap it up: Is there communication between states?

*

In The First Part we found that the state is redundant. This is a resultant observation and not an eternal one. Humanity clearly should not be viewed as an unchanging entity, and yet even with very intelligent people, history is viewed through an unchanging humanity; it views evidence of human activity in books and whatnot and sees change as something that occurs to this static thing called humanity.[44] It changes appearances, does different things, uses different languages and accents, has different technology, but "it" never changes; "it" is this entity that stays the same as change occurs around it or upon it. Perhaps this might account for why we have such difficulty in explaining the arrival of humanity on the scene of history; we have a quite weak ability to explain just *how* humanity came about: Our answers reflect our own ability to see ourselves in history, as the 'end product' of historical process.

Limitation shows itself everywhere and is symptomatic of the issue we face in philosophy. The main issue is how we speak of things – less how we *think* of things, and yet either manner leaves us in a state based upon itself, rounded out by itself on all sides, with nothing supporting it but 'thought-speech'. So the theorists tell us; so philosophy finds thus.

---

[44] Hence we have efforts of *post* and *trans* human and such theoretical contradictions.

The Event that we seek can be put into many frames; we can speak about it in many ways. Zizek quotes Alain Badiou:

> "...a contingency
> (encounter or occurrence)
> which converts into
> necessity: it gives rise to a
> universal principle
> demanding fidelity and
> hard work for the New
> Order." [45]

Badiou appears specifically political and quite often to follow the critical maxim that everything is political. I would agree, with the caveat that everything is political until it is not. His enjoys the hard sense of community and responsibility to society. If we read this alongside Kant, he is saying that which is already involved with society is necessary, that which society calls for in action for social justice is necessary, but that which demands fidelity, which is to say, the hard work, *involves the contingency* or that

---

[45] Zizek, p. 160.

which is not automatically implied by the (political) subject or by this converting into necessity. Again, the emancipatory subject and the potential for communication from the outside.[46]

---

[46] Badiou's book *Being and Event* has as its impetus how something can arise from nothing. His involved proof is how void, or the 'nothing' upon which philosophy finds itself, interacts or otherwise is able to be involved with or effect what is *not void*, or what could be called 'reality', politics, or what he calls "the multiple". His notion is that the void erupts into reality and begins an order of things. The basis for his ideal is that politics, or something similar, contains or otherwise *is* the totality of everything that can exist, but –to my eyes at least – his claim appears less ontological than logistical.

Emancipation

The question is oriented in two ways, each centered upon a condition; emancipation as the addressor, and as the addressee. The general question of communication is about *from* or *to*, but in the midst of the argument, often the specific question of emancipation itself is set aside: *What* is involved with the communication of emancipation?

We know that a revolution cannot occur so long as the state stays in power, which is to say, so long as the structural-mechanical binaries involved with the maintenance of the state are in effect. Zizek ends his book with a tentative answer.

> *"...in politics, a contingent*
> *upheaval (revolt) is an*
> *Event when it gives rise to*
> *a commitment of the*
> *collective subject to a new*
> *universal emancipatory*
> *project, and thereby sets in*

motion the patient work of
restructuring society."[47]

Notice how precisely Zizek uses language here. He does not define an Event as a political occurrence or situation; instead, he defines the condition under which a political upheaval is an Event. This condition is "the collective subject as (committed) a new emancipatory project".

Our premise is *nothing exists outside of discourse*. If this is the case then the manner by which we realize it beckons Wittgenstein's Collapse because if there is nothing outside of discourse, then there is nothing we can say about it, not even "nothing". If there is something outside of discourse that we can speak about, then we have missed the collapse through a centralized method of thinking, and we will go around again.[48] Here, though, we are engaged with an Event, specifically, the Event of the book of the same name.

---

[47] Zizek, p. 160
[48] See The First Part for this discussion.

If we can at least think about the category of thought as a containment, then it is possible to understand what we could be dealing with in thought. The manner that Zizek indicates this totally reckoned subject is the "collective subject". The idea that must correspond with this situation must reside in contradiction because of how thought occurs in a direction, particularly 'outward', always eschewing itself in the activity of itself. Yet, thinking about the containment evidenced by the very idea of thought or thinking necessarily shows us that thought cannot be what we think it is: It is something else. It is not 'thought', some *thing*, nor is it the content of thinking—and yet it *is* some *thing*. For a word, we must say that it is a site of contradiction. The manner that thought exists is at once to indicate itself not indicating anything but something else; though some have said that it is the site where two discrepant aspects of existence join, such as the site of mediation of Plato's Ideal and Real, or Hegel's site of synthesis, even to say that it is a site where two polemical idealities meet is to say nothing of thought but that it has just avoided itself. In short, if we are honest about what is occurring, we must say that it at least is a collapse of reason. It is not even a site, but it is, actually, the Event of collapse; or more precisely, the Event.

Then with even coming upon *any* event the obvious thing to ask would be, why is everything still there (or here)? Why is not everything absorbed into the black hole nothingness of the thought-Event?[49] If we are to stay with the mediating ideal of thought, then we must put forth a hypothesis, an argument as to why we might be able to come to this conclusion; for, if we do not, then the collapse is just another idea, thought, at most, unfounded, and at least another metaphysical speculation that everyone believes in like, say, *nothing.*

This is why we can say that the Wittgenstein Collapse actually split philosophy into two camps; it split what we call *dialectical* into two distinct and irreconcilable manners of coming upon the world. One that does not recognize the collapse proceeds as Wittgenstein was

---

[49] Or as Graham Harman has put it: Why has not everything clumped together into an indistinguishable mass?

putting forth more food for thought. This mode is the one that was taken for granted and assumed solute in its obvious and axiomatic grounding.[50] This is the same route that views human thought as a kind of 'agency of change' that is an integral part of the motion of the progress of history; this route implicitly relies upon a physical brain as it attempts to decide how this brain is able to present to us various qualified meanings of the actual universe (only thought; only discourse; only human knowledge; object-subject duality; science; etcetera). Ideas similar to Manifest Destiny fit in to this category as the qualified meanings represent types of inspired access. The Existentialism of Sartre and the questions and answers of the Frankfurt School were efforts to come to terms with *why* the progressive agent of change (for a term) did not work or might be able to work despite the evidence; why, for example, did the agent allow for the abuses of technology like The Final Solution of the Nationalist Socialists and ultimately the general modern war-state. Yet they also pondered how it might be possible to reintegrate this agent positively into the

---

[50] One is conventional philosophical Reason.

world. In a very general yet truthful way, the philosophies of the 20th century were attempts to reconcile, not what is dialectical, but what has emerged as a kind of 'dialectics of the dialectic', that evident split which occurred of what is dialectical by the collapse of direct knowledge.[51] The doubling down by

---

[51] What we are calling the Wittgenstein Collapse could also be called the failure of direct knowledge. Direct knowledge here implies an ability or capacity for knowledge to attain or otherwise gather information *from* an object that is distinct and separate from the thinker to which all Beings qualify. Wittgenstein's Collapse shows philosophy that its unified effort, of a sort of romantic Kantian-Hegelian conspiracy, cannot be known, that its knowing is ultimately a particular structural organization having no correspondence to any true thing—even to falling outside conceptual inventions by thinkers. A Kantian premise taken to its inevitable end, the Collapse occurs due to no necessary link occurring between the term and its object, or the subject and predicate (analytical-necessary knowledge), and because the alternate Kantian submission, *synthetical-contingent knowledge*, typically occurs through its analytical counterpart. This is to say that before the Collapse there was an implicit and common philosophical orientation upon objects which viewed reason in the potential of direct knowledge.

It is possible to understand this 'synthetical mistake' (an industrial by-product) as a contradiction that becomes suspended to allow a tension to build into the World Wars—an assertion over the truth—a last effort of asserting 'the truth' through interventional violence, how things should be according to 'logic' (a particular coupled identity of logic and thought) over how things actually are – that then is supposed to be deconstructed in the post-war 20th century philosophies. Late 20th century philosophies are characterized by the attempt to discover or otherwise uncover the presumed hidden aspects of the dialectic which seem to have lead humanity through such an obtuse experience of knowledge.

It is this 'typicality' that could not be noticed until all conceptual defaults were taken; every sense taken upon the assumption of the agency of thought had to be used up before 'typically' could be used and have meaning in this context, but it was with Wittgenstein that what is 'typical' became pronounced by an effective 'not passing over what we cannot speak of'. Before all the conceptual defaults around the necessity of thought were used up, we could only speak in the context of 'always'.

As a side, the philosophical idea of *Correlationalism* came out of this notice of the typical near one-hundred years later. Zizek speaks to this temporal phenomenon of developing knowledge when he says this apparently sure notion of the common thought of individuals can be understood as the coincidence of the Postmodern, Modern Feminism, social justice and racial equity movements, among others.

Needless to say, I am not making an argument that this particular conventional mode of Being is wrong or incorrect. It is a mode of Being, it cannot be incorrect. But when oriented in a project that proposes as part of its method a solution to be actually solute in its actuality, as opposed to grounded in suspended theoretical postures,[52] we are justified to point to the

---

that we cannot choose to change; change only occurs when there is no other option.

[52] I use *suspension* in a number of contexts through this essay; the precise meaning can be problematic. In general, I draw the analogy from chemistry; namely, a heterogeneous mixture with particles which are sufficiently large for sedimentation. The term, 'suspended theoretical postures' is meant to convey how the veracity of any theory is understood to be what 'settles', the 'sediment'. This is to say the 'sediment' is understood to indeed *be the proof* of the veracity of the proposal; i.e. it is self-evident, albeit argumentatively. This essay decries such methods but

behavior such a posture promotes or
encourages, even if it does not overtly
condone the appropriations, and indict it as
complicit to perhaps presenting itself in a
false light. We are allowed to describe the
subject on the table; all sorts of methods can
be suggested to address it, but ultimately,
the best doctor merely creates an optimal
condition for the body to heal itself.
Conventional philosophy, on the other hand
and often enough, wants to suggest to us that
it occupies the position of God, in this
respect, as if everything lay under its whims
– perhaps even the Devil![53]

----

nevertheless supports the fact that such postures do
indeed function to *do work*.

[53] Every non-theological philosopher would most
probably deny that they have made any assertions
about God whatsoever. In fact, I wager that most
philosophers would say they merely develop
arguments based upon thoughtful consideration of
observations and discussion, that they have no
ulterior motive. But the most obvious of questions
should be how philosophical discussions are
supposed to be speaking of *the* reality. We must ask,
what power is given to the philosophers to be able to
make proclamations about what reality and the world
is *for everyone*? If the answer is anything but the
common power of thought and reason, I would be

Difference

The answer we are looking for is just *different*. The Postmodern theorists[54] opened the door wide, but not wide enough; it was just wide enough to appear like a solution, but it was an eternal critique, what some philosophers have said is a gaping negativity. The ideal of discourse (Aristotle's efficient cause) has not given us a solution; rather, in fact, the solution that it did give merely widened the discrepancy it was attempting to solve. For example, realism can be viewed fallback into populist (political) philosophy. In real terms, then, the Postmodernist idealization of the discursive path leads to nowhere but ideological fantasy which then ends up supporting the ideology it critiques by showing the infirmity of the modern subject, as well as how many voices usually must give way to a One voice again ("rise up!" means "become one voice against the powers that

---

surprised. For, what is *this* power? Can it be any power but reason? What is reason doing?

[54] See The First Part for a discussion about this generality.

be").[55] No more wondering about the cry for something Real. Even while good and necessary things have come out of it, in the reaction to it we are still left with a kind of empty philosophical legacy. People are not stupid; the problem was that *difference* was allowed to become the *same* again, the idea of difference formed the backbone by which to conserve the state into a relativity of power justified for power's sake.

We have defined *political* as concerning the negotiation of power. Power can be said to be the difference *between* unequal positions. We will use the analogy of an electronic circuit at various times in this essay. A circuit is a closed loop of energy; electrons move in one direction in this loop, from where there is more (as excess of electrons, or "-") to where there is less (a deficiency of electrons, or "+"[56]). The energy

---

[55] Is it really such a surprise that the idea reveals more forms of idea which then function to support itself as the foundation of all that is allowed to exist? What a great idea!

[56] This is the proper scientific notation of the situation. Since electrons are negatively charged, the pole with the excess of electrons is noted a "-". This is in contrast to the early days of understanding

58

of that circuit can be said to be the motion itself of the electrons. Hence, for our analogy here, politics occurs 'between' as the negotiation of power. In order for there to be politics, energy must already be presently moving, but the only real way to measure, or notice, if indeed energy is present in the circuit is to form an intervention. For the case here, this intervention can be said to be *political*. What is political is not the 'poles' from and to which electrons move, neither is it the movement which takes place all through the circuit without intervention (which we can call the *economy*), which is the power itself. Politics thus relies upon not the movement of energy (power), but it can be said to be indeed the *negotiation* of the power derived by an intervention into the economy that is already there. Politics relies upon what we could call, with reference to the economy, an artificial division of motion; it requires a division to negotiate.

---

electricity, where the pole with the excess was noted as "+" because it was supposed to have more of the energy.

The Political Event

So, we can come back to Zizek's question.

> *"What are the chances of*
> *an authentic political*
> *event...in which the*
> *process is the undoing of*
> *past events?"*

We might want to rephrase it to get at what he might really be saying. *"What are the chances..."* he asks. Is it possible to have a *political* event, an intervention into the economic movement, that itself is the undoing of past interventions? Politics itself is, to use a more exact word, an imposition of negotiation; past interventions (in this case) must not have worked as an intervention because *we still are having the intervention* (politics); this is a truism and an identity: Politics is by definition a negotiation of different positions (of the energy economy). We hear echoes of philosophers who stay to the claim that everything is political, but this is the same as saying that the circuits exist because of or inseparably from politics, that nothing exists without an intervention. Does not this sound strikingly familiar? This is what the whole, or at least a very large part, of philosophy has always been concerned with: How is a thought upon an object possible?[57] What is occurring that allows for an *incorrect* assessment of the object? How is it possible that a person can behave incorrectly? These are all the same question, stemming from different instances of that same situation as it is presented by various limits and various openings.

The three interrelated questions then: Is there is an Event which can change this persistent problem, an Event which changes the protocol that informs what and how openings may occur as well as what and how limits are applied, an event which alters the very scaffolding upon which the world is presented as knowledge? How can we have an authentic Event, which is to say an Event which actually restructures the field by

---

[57] This is similar to the question "how does something arise from nothing", or perhaps more respective of the conjugation, "how does something communicate with nothing".

which the intervention(s) of the past have gained their meaning as political events? And by this Event not losing or negating their quality or ability to *be* political events as such, but rather altering that by which they have gained their stature as foundational and inseparable to that singular structure of truth we call reality?

It is not a far step to say that a circuit *is able to be* defined by the interventions though which we gain a measurement of the energy which flows through it; the identity of a circuit surely can be defined by the interventions, but it is not the same as saying that a circuit *is* that set of interventions.[58] We likewise can

---

[58] I offer a definition of an electric circuit for our analogy. A battery, or power cell, is not a circuit; it is a power source characterized by a power potential. The energy of a power source is only noticeable when the circuit is closed by connecting the positive and the negative poles. But not even this. The connecting of the two poles only evidences that power is present, often through heat, but there is no measure in the connection to find out how much energy. Yet, it can be said to be a circuit. In real power sources, the aspects of power are defined in its construction. For our analogy, though, the definition

of how much power is in the original source is moot (because it is imprentent and infinite). Our point then is that it is only in the intervention of components within this original circuit (electronic components such as capacitors, resistors, transistors, lightbulbs, switches, meters, etcetera) that a measure can be made as to how much or what kind of power is present. Also, at these interventions the measurement only finds what power exists between the intervention and another intervention. We call the series of interventions *reality* with the stipulation upon the analogy that it is not an ontological theory about what might be true of things. The analogy is only meant to be taken so far, for a specific use, and then dropped. The last application for its use then is to see that at no time is a real intervention able to surmise or come upon the total series of interventions by which to be able to assess what the actual universal reality may be. Unlike an analysis of an actual electronic circuit, the 'circuit of reality' cannot be viewed or come upon through an analysis of a total series of components because such an assessment would de facto be a measure of one intervention to another. This is to say that there is *only* religious theoretical proposals as to how the thought and the object of thought relate to derive a functional knowledge. Hence, the only way to come upon the 'total circuit' is to make a move which is contradictory to the real philosophical method. This move is thus not *summarily additive* so as to presume that a realization of the whole might be found

understand as true that if there is no measurement, no intervention by which to negotiate the power to get things done (by the way), then there is no circuit, but the question on the table asks if the circuit can still be a circuit if it does not rely upon the values that the defining interventions yield. Politics implies by its presence, and outright asserts its truth wherever we encounter it, the radical and transcendental truth[59] that

---

through a kind of reverse engineering of knowing.
We know what such reverse engineering finds:
Phenomenological Nothing and Spiritual-religious assertions of the true content of this Nothing, and its theological counterpart the political-ideology real power plays of identity.

On the contrary; what is contradictory to this real cosmological method is indeed to begin from that situation where no interventions exist, the original source of power through which all interventions determine their measure: What the real faith deems as heretical: Absurdity.

[59] This kind of truth is based in transcendence because the existence of another existing thing is said to be dependent upon the (a) first thing. This organization depends upon an inference of an encompassment which then holds the two 'in just that way' to allow only the first to reckon the second in such a way that the second can only then reckon the first through the first's privilege.

no *circuit exists* without the intervention, which is, without politics. By this assertion of ubiquitous dependence, the subject *is* the intervention, the subject *is* inherently and all times political[60]. Then, not only do we have to ask if this is the case under all conditions (what conditions can be changed? What are the conditions for which change is accounted for as change?), but what is occurring that the political event might *never* involve an alteration of the field by which it gains its authenticity as a political event. This is the question of the "last frame" later in this essay.

In the case of an economy that is punctuated by political interventions which do not only define the economy but indeed negotiate (define) the relations of power within the economy, we have to ask what this economy is which is defined solely by interventions? If we can ask this question, then the possibility of having a real economy without such interventions is *possible*. This

---

[60] This essay attempts to remove what is often posed as *radical* from the stakes by putting a finger on that apparent object which is usually too vague to be identified.

is in reference to Zizek's question "What are the chances..."; well, the answer is *no* chance. With reference to what politics is *doing* (which is defining by negotiating) there is no definitional chance that a political Event could occur which would change the parameters of the political economy. We see this everywhere; the institutions of modern society function to absorb what might be interventional to thus make such methods a part of the state of controlling the economy. The very term 'revolution' is now a part of the process of bringing into line elements that lay outside of control; the state uses revolutions to support humanity's existence, anything else is an ideological fantasy. Yet, within the economic flow into which politics breaks, there remains a *possibility* (as opposed to probability) that such a revolutionary and emancipatory project can and does occur.

The reckoning of such possibility of intervention must occur outside of what is political yet while retaining the political identity as a valid route of intervention. This is the question of the *frame*; what transpires for such a movement (a political intervention) has to do with the precise

origin of the intervention. From the strict frame of politics, we are supposed to imagine that interventions occur like jumping fleas; their jump is so powerful and high, the arc of their leap so great, we are to think that they begin with us, attain such a height as to have encountered a reality so different that their return to their source of food is actually an encounter from another dimension.[61] Might we ask, at what height do we define the atmosphere of reality? Unlike the previous philosophical paradigms which propose various types of ways to intervene into the intervention (to politically change politics), different 'entrance vectors', if you will, the idea of the frame does not involve the effort for conceptual reorganization. On the contrary, no reorganization can be made to occur; rather, the reorganization marks that atmosphere at which we are *required* to call for a reorganizing of sense or else be like the philosopher returning to Plato's cave.[62]

---

[61] A discussion of Joseph Campbell's work is forthcoming.

[62] The Allegory of the Cave is a famous story by Plato about a philosopher who is set free from the reality formed by shadows on a cave wall. A group of people are chained in this cave and made to sit only looking at shadows of the puppets that are drawn

So it is that what is common of the being of human requires a reality where subjective interventions occur. This is all good and well and is the reason why, if we are to speak about the truth of things, we must speak in a particular manner; it is not so much that we are required to prove the non-intervening status of the subject (or its ability to intervene, for that matter), it is more that if we are to describe what is occurring with the intervention, there can be no debate whether such interventions occur. The idea of the political intervention is able

---

across the light of the fire between and the cave wall and they understand this condition as reality itself; the cave dwellers thus understand these puppets' shadows are Real Things, not aware that they are merely shadows of actual things. The philosopher, freed from this situation, proceeds out of the cave into the light where she is able to view the actual truth of the situation. So enlightened and excited, she returns to the cave and tells the people there about this great truth of their situation. They do not believe her and ultimately kill her as a heretic or mad (who knows?). A contemporary interpretation of the Allegory would suggest that the philosopher never left the cave at all, that part of the being of human is to think that they have left the cave and returned.

to be addressed and disputed in all sorts of manners, but exactly the point where discussion accrues over the intervention there we have entered into the realm where such discussion has become moot. As we have said; the content of contradiction does not occur in argument, even while argument about the content may arise. Such a true discourse gives as it takes back.[63]

From the point of view of politics, that which has intervened was always an identity, but the looking is the waiting for what is 'out of this world' to inject itself through the otherworldly traveler to be food for his landing. This is known as mediation. Nevertheless, the consistency is the traveler never disjoined from itself nor not itself; if anything occurred it was the *realization* that what is reflective of political economy, that which *becomes* the real reference, is a 'lie'; this is to say it does not contain nor reflect all that exists, but actually reveals its partiality. We will get into the repercussions of this Event later; for now it is pertinent to notice that the political estimation of identity *does not* allow a consistency of subjectivity

---

[63] See The First Part.

outside of its intersectional identity; even as a subject may have seen something outside of the political atmosphere, the issue arises when the subject indeed views itself as having gained a novel view, of a knowledge that has been outside which now needs to be brought into the world. We often hear of this feat; we call it 'inspiration' in one instance, and 'intuition' in another, and the ultimate issue underlying all of it is communication. When the traveler has succeeded with his intervention from 'outside' it affirms that the political estimation of totality is correct because the field remains intact and unchanged.[64] Then we are left to ask what knowledge the traveler indeed came upon, and what exactly the intervention amounts to. What changes?

Psychoanalysis

We have a way of measuring the potential involved with the non-partiality of economic power without an intervention which negotiates a power differential; Zizek calls this *psychoanalysis*. Despite the

---

[64] And yet, everything is somehow different.

critiques from every angle against the Freudian as well as the Lacanian version (every version?), many of the complaints mounted against the Zizek version have not been "emancipated" from the territory carved out in history which establishes terms to their identities. This essay is an attempt to intervene into such a tradition by allowing for the all the critiques and rebuttals to stand as equally true in their potential to cause or otherwise be involved with political change. In fact, each comment upon psychoanalysis in whatever form has brought about some sort of political negotiation, whether it was large or small; the intervention here is to allow that such political critiques are true in their potential to intervene.

*

What is psychoanalysis? Without consulting any sort of historical or institutional reference, the simplest answer is an analysis of the psyche.[65] The benefit of

---

[65] I keep the term *psyche* to the most general sense. It is not merely *mind*, neither *soul* nor *spirit* nor *mentality, mental operations* nor *mental world*. The

a materialist proposal is that it takes this simplest of things to be self-evident. What this means in terms of our analogy above, is that through the view upon material *only* we are able to have a view of the whole economy. A political intervention, in this light, can be understood in the various contexts of itself, the various leverages of power, what may be at stake as well as probabilities of outcomes, yet whatever conventional scientific and critical modes can accomplish, the view of material can allow for it, but by this view no intervention is made. This is the opening of science: No opening is available, no philosophical ontological link; there is only a political link, which arises in various forms at various moments. Also and coincidentally, no intention can be discerned because the material reflects the power of the whole economy; what is intentional of such an intervention is also ultimately political. The contradiction inherent of this posing is why we can speak of what is *mistaken*. Here is the contradiction in terms: The political economy is unable to measure an intervention that is

---

most specific we can be for this founding term is to say it is that which occasions that which is occurring. The love of wisdom concerns that which is occurring.

not political. In our analogy of the electric circuit, it is as if the material intervention is the reading taken between poles – not component/interventional assessments – *before* politics can begin to determine and negotiate the terms of the circuit, or for a term itself, reality. Here we begin to understand the transition evident in Marx and the confusion that appears with subsequent discussion about his work.[66]

---

[66] Noted Members of the Frankfurt School and others had put forth an interpretation of Marxism that still others have argued takes Marx's work completely out of the context and spirit in which it was written. In the context of Zizek, oddly enough, we can call this change in the semantic register a change from materialism to materialism and it would seem to corroborate this essay to suggest that before the Wittgenstein Collapse, the 'undivided' world that rested on a 'single' form of dialectical understanding, was split into a sort of 'dialectics of the dialectic', as Theodor Adorno coined by the book of the same name, *Negative Dialectics*. The argument over which register of Marxist interpretation might be correct, which 'dialectical discourse' is being used in the assessment, is an example of the confusion that arises when the philosophical given is assumed to have passed through the Collapse unscathed, i.e. that *philosophy* encompasses all possibility in a unitive discourse.

This is to say that the intervention concerns the material economy, and not the political economy. The political economy can do what it does all the while not have an effect upon the material economy, which is to say they collude in effective Being. This explains how or why politics is understood to concern all that exists, i.e. politics is the determination of power in negotiation. The material economy does not negotiate; it *contains* sites of negotiation and can account for the activity at such sites, but itself is not involved in them, or, at least, does not have to be; there are repercussions of this for being human.

For our purposes here, however, the point is to see what is being identified and what is doing the identifying. What is being identified necessarily has a partial view; the totality of its view is mitigated by its investment of identity, which is a negotiation of power. Material, in this manner, is political material, material which must necessarily be divvied up, its value distributed among the circuit of identities that have interest in the negotiation.

The psyche should always be considered as a total presence. It does not begin as a total presence, but that which is before also exists before any investments have been made; before a total presence there is the economy. Here is the world, now the question is how it is dealt with: It is dealt with through the psyche.

Kant

The significance of Kant's formulations can be pertinent, particularly the *analytical* knowledge. Remember; here, the subject is implied in the predicate. Any judgment that is made about it must correspond with its presentation; any judgement which does not correspond with its analytical necessity is simply false. Of his four developments, i.e. analytical a priori, analytical a posteriori, synthetical a priori, and synthetical a posteriori, the second one, *analytical a posteriori,* is said to not exist because it is contradictory, but it is more sensible to say that it is merely correspondent, because the judgement based upon experience must correspond with the analytics of the statement; the justification of the proposal is contained in the experience of knowing what the proposal is. With his assertion of no *analytical a posteriori* propositions, Kant effectively imposes the cutting off of knowledge from experience. We find that the rest of his proposals flow out from this discontinuity of world and thought and that for the next two hundred and more years, still, philosophy attempted to work out how to get knowledge and experience (that is, worldly experience) back in bed together.

*

We might begin to understand why this philosophical paradigm of direct knowledge eventually collapsed when we notice the contradiction involved with Kant's centering his epistemological program upon the *synthetical a priori*: Because this is the development which is ultimately contradictory.[67] The rooting out the 'rational'

---

[67] In traditional logic the contradiction shows what is false, and by default, along what way the true answer must be sought. Here, though, with *thought* involved with the positing of 'the Reason', the scheme of Kant's four developments is understood to have *necessary* repercussions for *reasoning into Being*. For a bridging of science and philosophy, as well then to arrive at a science of philosophy, his loaded

repercussions of his program depends upon viewing the four developments as distinguished essentially, locating particular

---

and false judgement upon the *analytical a posteriori* shows thus that the opposite must be the way. But this way is based in nothing which can lead us back to actual worldly things 'that we experience'; the *synthetical a priori* is a judgement that is made outside of experience upon a situation that does not contain any evidence of itself for what it is. In the Kantian world things must therefore exist in an ideal sense, in the mind, and the mind must therefore be the designator of all things knowable as this knowing must be immanently connected to all existence (the term *empirical* is also in this same way confounded in Romanticism). Since the world in which we exist occurs by knowledge, we are ultimately led to be found within ideal constructs much of which develop or otherwise occur though *reason* in general, but the mechanism for this *reasoning* must be a manner to connect with something that is not specifically 'the thing in question' (because knowledge is knowledge for itself). This contradiction is mitigated through something that is thus *transcendental* to all things, the thinker included. So, the mediation which occurs between this transcendent and the thought is through *inspiration* and *intuition* of what is *Reasonable*. Yet, as we see now, all this kind of speculating occurs due to the simple initial denial of the obvious source of the contradiction: The unitive thinking subject.

instances which necessarily arise distinct unto themselves. We need only look at what he gives us in the Preface to the first edition of *The Critique of Pure Reason* to know that something went wrong in not only his appropriation of his work, but the subsequent extension that stretched out over the next one-hundred or so years. We can say, positively, that it was the political dimension which preoccupied this Reason with itself, the partiality that is the content of the contradiction: Of course, experience must come first, *but then* once reason takes over, we have to have an account for what reason is doing, and thus, in order to be sure, to have a generalizable science of reason, we must account for this reason. The *synthetical a priori* is a contradiction in terms that finds its solution in that which has been ostracized by the system, for the purposes of having a science of the system; we know now that this 'scientific endeavor' was never salvageable: the *analytical a posteriori* is the content of the contradiction erected by the *Pure Reason* through denial of what is necessary of experience. It is a play on words; a play that developed and continues in the develop of a theological following in the Continental tradition (at least), one that could not admit its theological bearings even after the Collapse of its basis for overtly consistent logic.[68]

Yet when we read Kant through this lens, we see that what he was writing, at least as his premises, says nothing different. We can see this in his next important idea: The *Categorical Imperative*. Without going into an extended argument, is it not now plain to see that this is nothing less nor different than the *analytical a posteriori*? It is a category that must and can only behave according the category.[69] Is this any different than saying that the subject is implicit in the predicate? But Kant would have this *imperative* as an ethical mandate, a manner by which to judge the ethics of an activity,

---

[68] The faith in direct knowledge.

[69] The *category* is a necessary parameter for his discussion of practical ethics. The *pure reason* of his position cannot be actualized from the stand point of ethical behavior, so the *categorical imperative* is a way to place the *pure reason* within the scope of the necessary view that involves how one ought to behave: In the ideal sense, one ought to behave according to the category that is presented. Material behaves according to the category presented at all times.

but further, as a kind of ideal for hope. What is ethics but based upon a choice that is made incorrectly, a choice that is inconsistent with the dictates of the category involved? But what choice was made? The choice of (pure) *reason* which is the denial of the content of the contradicting aspect of the system which is the practical and hypothetical systems.[70] Through the Kantian system we have an extensive analysis into ethics which yields an ultimately inconclusive manner by which to conduct any activity ethically: The process which develops itself into a universal exaltation of its own preeminence with Hegel, and then proceeds to fall apart under its own conceptual-real disjunction—this collapse to be asserted against—ultimately ends with an existence based on and in *nothing*.

---

[70] Kant juxtaposes the Pure Reason and the Categorical Imperative with Practical Reason and the Hypothetical Imperative. Contrary to the typicality of reality, through these categories he elaborates the contingency of the pure reason and the necessity of the practical reason. Ironically, in effect, he argues for the power of reasoned thought to create worlds, as we find in the Existentialist and Postmodern philosophies of the modern era.

The Psyche

What is the process and what are the results? The process must be located as a process of the psyche. Again, without consulting the historical tradition and remaining with the material before us, any consideration of a process of ideas must begin with a logic of the psyche.[71] For this logic, the ability to make sense of the kind this essay supposes to describe, we have to take into account two kinds of ability which are usually not considered except to posit one reconciliation. Such singular or unitive reconciliations we know as *philosophy*, but most often specifically ontology. Since conventional philosophy is more concerned with making ontological arguments than it is about addressing what may be true, we might begin to see that its methodological orientation promotes a particular kind of existence which is concordant with its implicit call for action; 'critical thinking skills' seems a more appropriate title to its activity than 'philosophy' proper. The conventional philosophical method is little

---

[71] We have already consulted the tradition; see below.

more than critical thinking which never confronts its apparent ability, and in as much forms the comment of this essay.

Critical philosophical thinking is all good and well and serves a vital purpose. Yet, the only way we might justify a proposal that conventional philosophy is nothing more than a regimen of critical thinking is to at some point cut off or interrupt the continuum that enjoins reality to thought. In order to be able to say with any truth that there is a kind of critical thinking that understands itself in the context of discussing what is true of reality—for example, that real discourses contain, reflect, represent or otherwise enforce a certain power differential or any semantic encoding—a partition must be erected in the world of thoughts, because in the activity of the analysis of real things the motion of the analysis itself is avoided as a real thing. If I am a subject of that real world then in order to maintain that the analysis is indeed also real, I must *realize* that there are two abilities of the psyche that are not reconciling.[72] If there is no partition, then I

---

[72] Or, are reconciling through a denial of a *pass,* which is to say, through *faith.* See below and The

82

find myself suspended in a world of relativity grounded in the first convenience of the True Object. To actualize this relativity, then, as opposed to merely having an intellectual conception of it, for my thinking I must first recognize that the ability to think critically about the world, in the end by extension to its greatest potential, leads to the conclusion of nothing.[73] Then, I must be able to connect that conclusion to the fact of my thinking without excuse, without a default that would suggest to me that my thinking yet is still able to come upon True Things of reality. I must fully admit that nothing supports the process of my thinking, which is to say, that thinking exists for itself and only for itself. I cannot, at this point, recourse to say "brain" or some sort of physical instance, nor at this point can I say "spirit" or "consciousness", because, for one, my reasoning has lead me to understand that there is no reasonable manner of connecting the object of my

---

First Part. Also, this is the significance of Kierkegaard's work.

[73] If it does not lead to nothing, then thought is invested of a faith, towards a common religious cosmology, and will go around the critical cycle again: The effort of critical thinking argues its own legitimacy as self-evident.

thoughts with any actual object, abstract, concrete or of any qualification whatsoever,[74] and, because recourse to a transcendent, as yet unknowable, aspect of reality is merely another manner of denying that the conclusion of reason is nothing. I cannot retain the consistency of the thinking subject and still entertain the idea that I am thinking something true. I *can* have any sense about it I want, though. What is sensible is that my thinking will one day produce a solid linking from thought to object of thought, and indeed that this thought has a solid ground, but we will find that as soon as I apply reason to this presumption of continuity, I have recourse to one or another mode of *passing* an assailable gap in the capacity of thought. I must actualize this *pass* as a foundational feature of the ability of the psyche to come upon both true and real things. Yet, once this impasse has been actualized, recognized and accepted, once I have brought this impasse out of the ideal world of concepts and into the actual world of the psyche, I have, in effect, allowed for the

---

[74] In other words, there is no reason why reason is reasonable except as it can be involved with a direct knowledge.

totality of the material economy to be
realized for what it is: True.

The Collective Subject

Returning to Zizek's statement. If I
have not been explicit until now, here it
seems prudent and fair to introduce a
criterion that often enough seems foreign to
philosophy; this criterion is *simplicity*. When
we look at some of the big names of
philosophy, often enough the explanation
they give which moves us into their ideas are
pretty simple. Wittgenstein is a good
example; even without a working knowledge
of complex mathematics or a studied
historical knowledge of philosophical ideas
his *Tractatus Logico-Philosophicus* can be a
pretty simple book for the layman; that is if
one reads it *as* a simple statement.[75] The
preface begins:

> *"This book will perhaps*
> *only be understood by*
> *those who have them-*

---

[75] One could make an argument that the *institution* of
philosophy is invested in keeping people from
understanding simple ideas.

*selves already thought the
thoughts which are
expressed in it—or similar
thoughts."[76]*

What are we to make of this, the
first sentence of his one and only book?[77]
Applying the principle of simplicity we can
say that what he means is that those who
have already had such thoughts will
probably understand him and those who
have not most likely will not.[78] What a
simple statement. Yet, by the principle of
conventional philosophy, what he is saying is
that those who are so steeped in the trenches
of scholarly verse will understand him. I
doubt this. I perhaps will secure my place as
forever ostracized by the academy of
philosophers, or at least laughed at in saying
that I doubt if hardly any learned

---

[76] Ludwig Wittgenstein, *Tractatus Logico-
Philosophicus*.

[77] The other book attributed to Wittgenstein,
Philosophical Investigations, was published after his
death.

[78] It is well known that Ludwig did not expect *most
people in general* to understand his philosophy.

philosophers understand him, and this because the principle of conventional philosophy seems to be "nothing is as it appears, and that which is most complex and involved with densely concave opacity must be true". Take another example from Wittgenstein's book:

"The world is everything that is the case."[79]

Can there be a simpler expression of truth as a definition maxim, but also as the beginning of philosophy: *The world is everything that is the case.* Is there *any* philosophical paper from any institution in our current day that begins anywhere near to this kind of simplicity? I would venture to say no; most philosophers begin with positioning themselves within ideas, discourses and authors that have already been discussed. I am pretty sure in Ludwig's 75-page book he does not site one philosopher (but maybe a couple a mathematicians though).

---

[79] *Tractitus Logico-Philosophicus*, Statement 1.

But let's back up a little. Here is Descartes, from his *Meditations on First Philosophy*:

> "*I shall now close my eyes,*
> *I shall stop my ears, I*
> *shall call away all my*
> *senses, I shall efface even*
> *from my thoughts all the*
> *images of corporeal things,*
> *or at least (for that is*
> *hardly possible) I shall*
> *esteem them as vain and*
> *false; and thus holding*
> *converse only with myself*
> *and considering my own*
> *nature, I shall try little by*
> *little to reach a better*
> *knowledge of and a more*
> *familiar acquaintanceship*
> *with myself.*"[80]

Can you bring to mind *one* philosopher alive today who has expressed anything near to this kind of honest approach? Never mind if we already know what Descartes had to say in the rest of this

---

[80] René Descartes; *Meditations on First Philosophy*, Meditation 3.

book, whether it is right or wrong or what his point is. Who today comes into philosophy with this kind of willing naiveté? No one; or if they did or do then it was when they were children, who then, upon entering the university are basically often keel-hauled into *not* being naïve and open to possibility. By the time they might come upon the idea to be so open, I would wager that many if not most see such openness with reference to what has already been said, and by default, what they have been taught or exposed to. *What are the chances* that such a student would be able to set aside – if they even would want to – what they have been taught? Even if they could, such consideration of *firsts,* I would bet, would be in reference to what other philosophers have said about such firsts; their *first* usually ends up being a *second, third, fourth, fifth...*in the long lineage of where firsts are supposed to start according to the discipline.

Of course, this is not to suggest that such students are incorrect in any sort of philosophical activity they are involved in, including myself. To say *conventional* should not be an insult; it should be a way to honestly identify what kind of philosophy is being done. One quick way to find out is to view that first statement; if a question comes to mind about what he means by "world", then most likely the reader is one of the people who he figured would not understand what he is saying. Simple; fact. My point here is to show where people are being honest, and not to indict people for being wrong. There is no wrong here; there is only *kinds*. There is only an opening of space.

To get back to our point; such a pointing finger is being used to indicate what is partial, what is founded in the—what we now call the *capitalist*— political economy. Look at our two examples of simplicity; are they saying the same thing? This is a pivotal question. The two answers are yes *and* no. And, the answer that is come to is not exclusive to the other so as to demand from the other a relinquishing of status or a reduction to *false*. This is not *either/or*;[81] it is

---

[81] The discussion about the ramifications of Kierkegaard's book *Either/Or* occupy the topic of another essay. For now, it is enough to say here that while we question reason and thought it is the strict adherence to *any* particular ideological system which brings about the critical discussion of which Kierkegaard brings to notice. That is, it is not *only*

indeed a functional and quite effective (as opposed to false and rejected) *and*. The answer is yes and no. What this means is that the answer which argues itself is a *type* of answer that reflects a particular orientation upon things, or an *orientation upon objects*, as we will get to.

Of course, we can see that Ludwig and René are not saying the same thing because Ludwig is saying something about "the world", and Rene' is talking about his personal approach. But what if we switch these designations? What do we get if Ludwig was showing us an approach on things, and Rene' was telling us something about "the world"; what if Ludwig was not actually talking about "the world" but was giving us the manner by which philosophy should proceed to discover truth. Rene',

---

the Western Christian ideology, but *every* ideology which begins to look into its own internal functioning. The idea that the content of Kierkegaard's *Either/or* is specific to Christendom is itself an ideological *either/or* designation. Regardless of what critical move it wants to make it would be a distinctly political move toward asserting a proper reality.

likewise, could be telling us about the world, that the world is "closed" and "silent" and little by little lets us be more acquainted with our relationship with truth. Ludwig perhaps was telling us what exactly is the case, and Rene' something about how truth works.

We will not explore those entrances further here because it is enough to notice how the political economy functions to grant ways into discourse: The common manner by which to enter a discourse is to assume that the terms reflect identities that are being fashioned in such a way to deliver distinct and particular objects of knowledge to our knowledge-thoughts. In general, if a different set of terms are used and or presented through a different clausal structure then the phrase is *meant*—but more than mere meaning—to be reflecting particular and essential identities that are distinct by virtue of the evidence of that clausal variation. In other words, terms are taken to be interventions into the economy that is being defined by that greatest set of interventions.[82]

---

[82] The catch is that this 'greatest set' can never be found but is always presumed. This deferment of

So, when Zizek talks about the "collective subject" above, the assumed meaning is that set of interventions which takes place in the eternal "circuit" that is the political economy. The individual real people who all have opinions, voices and bodies.

The uncommon, or the manner which understands, for example, Ludwig and René as talking about the same thing, is that view which does not in its nature intervene in the political economy, as we described earlier. It is that manner which has the world as its case, which, in the terms of René is *true*.

*

Psychoanalysis, in Zizek's terms, is that which concerns the psyche, and the psyche is that which determines the world. The world is the case. The first philosophy is

---

what is impossible into possibility is the *transcendental clause*; that which allows that set of political identities to have substance as real things. Later we will discuss this in terms of the Master Signifier.

that which takes account for the responsibility the psyche has for the world. This world has no interventions, nor can be intervened upon, but indeed presents the whole situation of the economy of subjects. If we do not take account for that which the psyche is responsible as the world, then we have to negotiate power through interventions. This happens all the time, though, so to suggest that something needs to be corrected due to an uncomfortable presence is really suggesting little more than there is an anxiety that is equivalent to a specific need for action to dissolve it; which is to say, a call to political action (a political event) as opposed to a call towards disrupting the political field (an authentic political Event).

So, again; the idea that this is presenting a choice, an argument that needs to be resolved as to how the psyche might be incorrect or how the world of the subject is 'but one world' in a multiplicity of worlds of subjectivity, is a political idea. When the world is the case, it does not mean that 'every subject has its own world that therefore becomes the case for that individual subjectivity'. Yet neither is it proper to say that 'there is only One world' or that 'consciousness is the whole of the existence'. These types of phrases are overdetermined in the intervention that is involved with being a political case, the world *of politics* attempting to come to terms with what is essentially *not* political. The key discernment here is that while the tension itself is entirely political, the *elements of* the tension are not *both* political. With this, we might now begin to understand a little better the meaning of Laruelle's non-philosophical position when it is placed along side of Badiou's, which then is also *not* the meaning of each individual argument. These two philosophers grant us the parameters of the case; Laruelle takes the phenomenal negativity to the total possible extension of positivity (unilaterally dual but not partisan), and Badiou attempts to merge the discrepancy (partisan politics defined by non-partisan eruptions of subjectivity that begin linages of ideology). Laruelle keeps the situation of what I call The Two Routes pure, while Badiou propose to solve the contradiction-in-argument by reducing essentially different aspects into one political-social frame: Void is kept as a founding essence, which then by faith invested of the (his) act[83] to inscribe or otherwise make by the effort or activity of discourse what is nothing *actually and in its completion* void—by the immanent subjective act of his Being he actually proposes as he offers the *object in-itself*, which then occurs or otherwise manifests along two irreducible routes, i.e. the Being that is Alain Badiou occurring in discourse in no other way than it can and does, and the Being that is the inscription (description, discourse) itself—then erupts into the multiple. For Badiou, subjectivity is the site of eruption, exactly where nothing exists or occurs until that site erupts into (political) Being, while with Laruelle no possibility of eruption ever occurs. Indeed, Badiou can admit as much when he is revealed to his orientation upon things; this may be the case for a while, but only in as much as it is only the case in a specific and argumentative

---

[83] The act of keeping fidelity to the truth. Badiou tells us that the operator of truth must relinquish the truth by virtue of fidelity to it; Laruelle, on the other hand, suggests that the truth is upheld at all times. When we understand the dilemma that the Postmodern authors noticed (but Lyotard in particular), then it becomes less difficult to understand the question Laruelle and Badiou have addressed.

moment. Nonetheless, Laruelle and Badiou are both correct.

The world that remains the case despite what reductions (interventions) are applied to it is the world that Zizek writes about through the trope 'psychoanalysis'. This is the Event itself where by everything attains meaning (truth, psychoanalysis); in the reckoning of what responsibility the psyche has for the world, all that is able to exist occurs in the collective subject (the case, the world). This situation then gives rise to a notice that communication of this situation is exceedingly difficult because it perpetually indicates the contradiction involved with such a view.

Revolution and Communication

With this non-singular, uncommon and, frankly, ante-revolutionary view, two consequences occur which, occurring together, is a sign of the psyche coming to terms with the Event. In time, we can understand orientation paradigms. The first indication is always a sense of difference, that this moment has a profound significance, that this moment is revolutionary and must be communicated 'to the masses'. In the One reality, or conventional orientation, where experience is reduced to what must be common, this is often understood at minimum as inspiration, and in the more extreme register, as a spiritual experience. The analysis of this moment finds a precipitate falling out of its immediacy (sediment falling out of suspension) which is the notice as well as the catalyst to divergence from conventional reductive and contradiction-phobic philosophy, and distinction in orientation. As a true Event such analysis (of a spiritual-type) cannot be generalized into a common human form because it is de facto bi-furcated along lines of emancipation, i.e. there is no chance of an authentic political event which changes the field by which past events have occurred, and, the authentic political event indeed changes the field by which all events are reckoned. The precipitate occurs along the lines of partition, of Barthes "cut",[84] such

---

[84] Roland Barthes, *The Pleasure of the Text*. He compares the pleasure of the text in a revealing along a cut of clothes; the arousal occurs along the line between the bare flesh and that which covers it. In another sense, say of Kierkegaard, the cut *is* the

that the consideration of plurality of individual subjects marks a complete contradiction (an intervention upon an intervention that would change the condition whereby interventions take place); out of the collective subject, falling aside of this line, as opposed to riding the ironic fence,[85] so to speak, the new emancipatory project may take form.

The second indication occurs when an attempt is made to communicate this situation of falling to one side (which is outside; a falling off). Only two results can come out of the attempt; they are correspondent with the emancipatory partition (above): Communication occurs or it does not occur; the predictable repercussions are correspondent with what happens: True.

---

anxiety of the coming upon irony and being sustained within it as a 'fall' to one side which is into the absurdity which is outside of the universe.
[85] Politics depends upon the subject of irony. It is the political subject in the attempt to assert or otherwise speak its identity which opens the door to partial interpretation of identity that thus remains in a state of perpetual negotiation.

Faith is the determination that the communication is or will be successful. If the communication occurs, then no emancipatory Event can be evident, for the sense it has is consistent with the expectation of sense, or what is sensible. This with the caveat that, according to the political effect where nothing happens apolitically, the emancipatory event is merely another event with various meaning in various moments and situations, having significance to the parties involved in different ways. For example, the election of a Left-wing candidate may announce to some that things have or finally will change, to others it may indicate that currency will become more valuable or may depreciate, yet while to still others it means more of the same. Granted that with such an election, there will be policies that will indeed be ground-breaking, will allow for exceptional social sectors to see more wealth flow and others less, and ultimately will confirm that the system is functioning and intact. In short, various events in reality will unfold; we thus make a correlation between *reality* and *faith*; in the statement "faith makes true", faith is that which allows for reality to appear cohesive in an actual and functioning manner; faith is a particular ordinance of *passes*, that which allows the *pass* to operate. If the Event is understood to have been communicated intact, that is, successfully, then faith is upheld as its theological tenants stay reflexive, showing the truth of themselves in the further potential of communication.

There is no question of reality here, no availability to find what is 'really going on' with reality due to the effectiveness of faith. What is really going on in reality will be found through real measures. The individual is not separate from reality nor is caught in an illusion of reality; the real identity of the individual cannot be separated out from the real political economy. The subject of such communicative event functions through an axiom of belief and the ability for belief to reflect true things and the successful communication of the evental revelation confirms the truth of faith. What we could call The Prophet of the Event in the act of communication thereby understands that his reflection of subjects are believing his revelation, and this observation then serves to verify the revelatory event itself.

Nevertheless, upon analysis of this type of emancipatory event such revelation shows itself to have intervened in the political economy in a manner no different than any other kind of intervention. This is a theoretical basis for the death of God and the foundation for the belief in the effectiveness of believing, as well as the notion of multivocality, the notion that individual subjects each have unique experiences in reality, etcetera. Reality thus is the arena which allows for a completion of sense in religious institutions and their congregants on one hand, and the modern nihilistic citizen on the other; all events engage in and become involved with the continuum of real events, what we call 'normalization'. Again; this description is not discounting or otherwise suggesting that this manner is not functional and in this way *true*; it is *real*. This is a description of the situation.

What happens if the communication does not occur? Orientation upon objects is a significant variable. Where no orientation is observable, the imperative of the Event will signal a continuing effort to communicate; orientation arises out of the final effort, out of the signal that is the emancipatory Event, the failure of the political economy to contain or otherwise represent all things truly. The failure cannot be a coming to understanding through reductionist political tactics, for then the failure has achieved a success in definition and therefore in establishing or communicating its identity.

The failure in this final regard is the Event which restructures the field in which the failure occurs, not into or towards another positive political reduction, but exactly another frame in which politics resides that we have called simply the economy. This Event amounts to a new universal emancipatory project: The communication of a fault in the structuring of reality that does not fall back into relative discursive negotiation.

This fault cannot be communicated directly because, by its very nature, it is a change in view that notices that the past is being changed at every potential juncture. The way this happens is similar to stubbing one's toe; less an accident, the activity cannot be prevented through any sort of thoughtful consideration of events, neither be avoided through any sort of discussion about it.[86] The only communication that can be said to be effective concerning the actual Event itself is one of verification rather than negotiation, of presenting the case to find out if another person has experienced the same thing on one hand, but indeed *presenting the case because another is validated* on the other; any other discussion about it would de facto not be concerning the authentic Event itself but the usual political negotiation of the identity of the event. In this way, the act of viewing an Event embodies the change in the nature of the Event; that is, the communication of the nature of this change cannot be witnessed by real political subject-identities because of their investment in the constancy of reality, the political economy. The communication of the authentic Event is

---

[86] That is, unless a person were to take on a behavior which, for regular human purposes, is completely unnatural; for example, making sure that every step one takes is noted consciously, making the act of walking entirely cognitive, or wearing shoes at every occasion, including in the ocean, in bed, in the shower, etc... Still, despite all the energy put into preventing – or on purpose for that matter – the stubbing of one's toes, inevitably it will happen again, somehow.

thereby not commonly understood for its truth, but instead verifies the that the paradigm, i.e. the political world in which such discourse takes its place, is true by its real designation. It is this political trick, the discursive sleight-of-hand that occurs with the more extreme investments in the transmutation that is real identity which organizes the condition for the potential of religious fundamentalism and spiritual zealotry.

*

Zizek appears to understand this dynamic without ever attempting to shine a light directly on it; psychoanalysis is a sufficiently malleable and flexible form through which to stand directly in the middle of things, without a call of mediation for the analysis. He speaks politically using the tropes "left" and "right", meaning the colloquial liberal and conservative parties:

*"...in the years of
prospering capitalism, it
was easy for the Left to
play Cassandra, warning*

that the prosperity was
based on illusions and
prophesizing catastrophes
to come..." now there are
protests and revolts
everywhere and the Left
has no response... no
suggestion of how to
"transpose islands of
chaotic resistance into a
positive program of social
change...we have dwelt in
a pre-evental situation
where an invisible barrier
seems to prevent a proper
Event, the rise of
something new.[87]

This invisible barrier is exactly which divides the political from the economical, the partition which cuts the Kantian Reason as well as the Marxist Revolution, each unto themselves, into two irreconcilable states of knowledge. In the terms of Laruelle's Nonphilosophy, this is called a *unilateral duality*.

---

[87] Zizek, pp. 160-161

Capitalism

Zizek is noted for telling us about the difficulty in even imagining outside of capitalism. This difficulty can be understood in how capitalism is a *political economic* state. An analysis of Marx would be appropriate here[88] but extraneous. Suffice it to say that not only is it quite difficult (if not impossible) to imagine outside of capitalism, but it is also quite difficult to imagine capitalism without democracy (that is, except as each can be perfect semantic emanations: Ideals).

In its purest sense, capitalism is an economic system that relies on the exchange of goods as the value of the good[89] is decided through a negotiation of the parties involved. How or why this value arises is not important as much as the awareness that the capitalist value indeed is not inherent to the good itself. Note in Marxism the value of

---

[88] Dialectical materialism is the Marxist form.

[89] For this discussion, a 'good' will be equivocal with 'labor' and 'work'; the point is the same regardless and will be used interchangeably.

revolution is in its ability to *contain* or *limit* value *to* the good; the entire structure of Marxist theory collapses in absence of the out which holds the value to the good within the parameters of the revolution *not enacted*; this is an analogue of scarcity and forms the basis of the ideal of supply and demand. Without a possibility for an out, that is, for some outside element which bestows value into a good that is beyond negotiation (in the case of Marxism it is *revolution*), all goods become valueless, or, they become valued for what they can supply—be—in themselves.

So far as such goods are not constituted by an innate value that is fixed to the use they serve, they thus have a value for the use they are put to; the defining of this use is found through the negotiation and the result of the negotiation is the political identity of the good, the relative power it contains.[90] For example; a tire can be used as part of the mobilization of a car, but it can also be a swing, as well it could be a habitat for an animal, the substrate for a children's playground, or the sole for a sandal.

---

[90] This is the definition of *fetishism*.

Whatever its use, its identity is inseparable from it.

There is no modern capitalism without a democratic involvement by virtue of the fact that some of the path that is travelled for the determination of the value of the good must be a negotiation by parties that have recourse to a revolutionary state, a *pre-evental* situation, a state which does not exist, is not real, nor is even findable,[91] where identities are free from the imposition of value; in other words, a *transcendent ideal*. It is the assumption of such access to freedom that allows for the negotiation of value to behave according to a perceived real veracity, that is, as though the good is indeed manifest inherently with that value. Nonetheless, it is not *merely* a matter of any physical system creating worlds or semantic models for itself; the idea that a physical system is able to accomplish such a feat is merely another ideal formed in the political negotiation.

---

[91] Through an act of will one can only find a pre-Evental situation through a redefinition of discourse, which means what is found is nothing; a route. See The First Part.

*

This is the triumph of capitalism: Investment and indebtedness. So ubiquitous to existence these qualities seem it is near impossible to see past them.[92] This paradox is due to the life that capitalism has allowed us to assume; Gilles Deleuze and Félix Guattari wrote about how capitalism usurps all value into itself and transforms objects into other objects right before our eyes. In a very real sense, capitalism is the state of the event, where all events are of equal footing and dependent on the result of negotiation. Zizek puts this phenomenon in terms of how identities with a fixed relative value (workers are workers who sell their labor to the capitalist boss), have become entirely liquidated such that the state itself is not merely supported by its citizens, but indeed more so the citizens have all become capitalists, each maintaining their own 'state business' or business of the state; everyone realizing that they are able to negotiate for

_____

[92] Again; the only way to get past them is to posit an absolute knowable transcendental idea; that is, an idea that is not merely an idea.

the value of their own work, the worker now determines her own use-value, negotiating her own terms of surplus value, values which can range sometimes day to day or task to task depending on the state of the political economy for the moment. The worker is an "entrepreneur of the self"[93] who invests in the state because the state supplies the route through which she identifies her value.

Investment becomes a good analogy for why the emancipatory event is always held at bay, why despite best intensions the frame by which emancipation might occur reduces the Event back into a *pre*-evental (a political event that occurs before politics) situation.[94] Capitalism is an economic system of excess, and this excess attains from the negotiation of power, or its economic sibling, value; the idea behind investment is to get more value from that same unit of investment. Value is power; value is the transmutation of the energy of the system to a determination of its contingent power, and

---

[93] Zizek, p. 161.

[94] In order for this to work, for an emancipated political subject to be free, a restructuring of the sense of history becomes necessary; i.e. an Event.

111

thus a measure conversion of energy into work. The significant question is *why*? Because, the ultimate goal of investment is to get more value out of the same work, to make it appear that the same amount of energy is doing more work. Then *how*? Energy is always conserved, no? It must be power then. The transmutation of this value is what Marx calls the power of the *fetish*, the 'magic' that is the gravity well for investment. Investment is also a way to use the excess value gained through the transmutation of power to do work on its own and this is the power of *debt*. As the investment pays off, the excess is again transmitted into political value; Zizek calls this kind of activity "openly ridiculous excess" because it is an excess that is generated purely in the mind, and yet nevertheless has the tangible feature of creating more value without work. This would be all good and well if at some point we could wipe the ledger because then the identity would serve its cardinal use (for having sense) over its ordinal (of power) use and our world might be, at least, a more sensible place.

The obscenity of capitalism is that as debt is accrued the debtor is not expected to pay it all back; in other words, the power generated by the mind resists *realizing* the truth of its products. In fact, everything starts to go terribly wrong when the debt is paid in full. The real aim of lending money is the indefinite continuation of the debt: The development of a relationship of "permanent dependency and subordination".[95] Not only is this a systemic mandate and assumption of debt, but it develops a particular kind of ideological posture which discourages and indeed will enforce the non-payment of the debt. Zizek's example is the International Monetary Fund; when Argentina was going to pay off their loan ahead of time, the IMF "expressed its worry that Argentina will use this new freedom and financial independence from international financial institutions to abandon tight fiscal policies and engage in careless spending."[96] Banks, the main institution of interest holding, indeed, are based upon the principle that all the money

---

[95] Zizek, p. 163.

[96] What else is this but a worry that Argentina would actualize ideological freedom, a principle which is supposed to remain suspended and *never* realized?

that is owed to them will *not* be paid back at one time. There is an invested interest allowing for no way out; this institution of political economy strives for its own expanded replication through its real principle of identity: An obligation that can never be met.

Indeed, what are the chances...

Authenticity

Zizek asks how we are to get out of this ridiculous situation, and one answer he offers is to drop the myth of the Great Awakening when the "dispossessed multitude [whatever] will gather its forces to make a decisive intervention".[97] Yet, similar to the meaning of the collective subject, we should not be so quick to point to the multitude of individual thinking people. Of course if we are speaking politically then we are referring to the group of dispossessed people; but this essay is about the Event which authentically structures the political field, and we are finding even as we just begin that this cannot be done, that the suggestion itself is a contradiction, and that the very idea is based in an unrealizable ideal, and that where it does occur it amounts to nothing less than an event like any other real event, good, bad, indifferent,

[97] Zizek, p. 163.

or emancipatory in its effect to use political identity. This is the full context of the authentic emancipation to which Zizek replies "it aint never gonna happen!"[98]

*

The reason for this short in the circuit can be understood with reference to the nature of the dialectical process. The dialectical process itself is a transcendent operation, born of an idea.

> *"A dialectical process begins with some affirmative idea towards which its strives...yet in the course of this striving the idea itself undergoes a profound transformation (not just a tactical accommodation, but an essential redefinition) because the idea itself is caught into the process,*

---

[98] Zizek, p. 163. We might add, *in* reality.

*(over) determined by its
actualization"[99]*

The point Zizek is making here is
that the quest of the idea is nothing more
than for itself, for the sake of the idea,
nothing more or less. Along this path,
though, before the subject comes upon the
non-identity of the idea (embodiment), the
subject routinely comes upon the idea in a
reflection which at first is not acknowledged
as a reflection, the coupling understood to be
that object with which the idea must grapple
in order to find the substance of the idea. It
is *this* idea which amounts to the retention of
the value of political identity, the capital
investment.[100] The affirmative idea is the
idea in question that must exist; it is the
invitation into the world. The idea and its
object draw the identity into the world
through this course such that the course and
the world become inscribed into the idea as

---

[99] Zizek, p. 164. Quote of Hegel from *The
Phenomenology of Spirit/Mind*.
[100] It is this investment which later 'disappears' or
transforms into an illusion. This 'miracle' creates the
demand for the subject to not pay back the debt (it
was an illusion) and maintain the fantasy at all costs
(for real).

117

real-truth, the manner by which reality occurs and exists everywhere and all-ways. This is a difficult if not impossible condition to overcome because the idea perpetually pulls back to reveal its object as some (any) point. This point then becomes a marker of truth, a plot point in the true existing world. That this marked truth is still an idea is not very appetizing for the identity being drawn, so at some point the subject will grow sufficiently content with the world that has been plotted. This is all to say that at some point the truth is found and the process is understood to go on about these found True Things, around them, in process a part of which the object has shown itself to not be.

In the story of the Event, in the occurrence of the Event, the journey of the idea towards its object becomes known for what it is, namely, an idea of process yet over-determined in its actualization; over-determined due to the precipitation of the True Object out of the idea.

It is the finding of the True Object that demands justice,[101] because the object

---

[101] See The First Part: Lyotard.

found seems to continue to avoid a strict observance of its trueness, or what it has been supposed of its truth: It is not recognized as the True Object of its description as there is always debate, negotiation and compromise of its found Truth. At this stage the object which precipitates from its idea is that *this* is the nature of reality, that the object reality is a negotiated truth, that the truth of the universe is a human universe, of human knowledge only. Laws are defined and negotiated as the subject attempts to justify the True Object in the name of her identity; process becomes a true aspect of the universe and methods of negotiating truths upon truths form a theoretical scaffolding of reality which argues itself against the tide of ideal process.

An authentic political emancipation is not emancipation from political identity; the most obstinate aspect of authenticity is that emancipation must have a corresponding True Object. In this manner The Truth of emancipation which concerns identity always occurs in the political world, so to suggest that there be yet an emancipation that changes the manner by which we reference change appears to be a bad investment because the sense to be had is that all the investments up till that point will then be worthless. Since identity and investment go hand and hand, this kind of emancipation seems like it would be a disaster.

From the view or orientation of the One universe and its True Objects, it is indeed a disaster, but only because of the over-determined manner by which the view is ordering real estimations. This is the reason why the Left is seen to not be able to come to any sort of effective organization toward emancipatory politics: Because they have come upon the contradiction of their method, the 'next' precipitate of their ideology should *naturally* be emancipation, but they are finding that this is not the case. What comes naturally, on one hand, is thinkers occupying a sort of 'space of doubt' about their theoretical existence and the work of knowing as though there is a real-truth as well as a right-way to the theory of existence. Then on the other hand, we have pockets of effective anarchy, of acting out due to and against the ideal restraint, the push back that is occurring because this last ideal will not relinquish another (its last, or in the last instance) True Object: The emancipatory subject. And the reason why it will not relinquish this (subject-) object is because all True Objects so far along this journey have come about through choice upon reason, which is to say, referring to our earlier discussion about Kant, upon the *synthetical a priori* and irony—irony will not be cornered to reveal its real-truth. We already know about the inconsistency in the affirmative intuiting Reason. So Zizek suggests that the way we allow for the emancipatory subject to arrive is to drop the ideal about it having to come to pass.

This most likely will not bring about an authentic political emancipation (there is no chance) because the idea of the political economy is based in all events being equal in probability (equal in the potential to be subject to chance). The necessities and real demands of life require that the ultimate justice for the True Object be set aside; the call for justice itself is thus transformed in the application of the necessary process to get things done. This new universe of failure thus evidences the two routes mentioned earlier. As Zizek says,

121

*"This new universality is
not an all-encompassing
container, a compromise
between disparate forces;
it is a universality based
on division"*[102]

This new universe occurs through
two routes, or evidences two orientations
upon objects.

---

[102] Zizek, p. 164.

Bibliography

Adorno, Theodor. 1966
    Negative Dialectics.
Badiou, Alain. 1988
    Being and Event.
Barthes, Roland. 1973
    The Pleasure of the Text.
Deleuze, Gilles, and Felix Guattari. 1980
    A Thousand Plateaus.
Deleuze, Gilles, and Felix Guattari. 1972
    Anti Oedepus.
Freire, Paulo. 1970
    Padagogy of the Oppressed.
Harman, Grarham. 2007
    On Vicarious Causation.
—. 2002
    Tool Being.
Heidegger, Martin. 1927
    Being and Time.
Kant. 1781
    The Critique of Pure Reason.
Kierkegaard, Soren. 1843
    Fear and Trembling.

Laruelle, Francois. 1996
Principles of Non-Philosophy.
Meillassoux, Quentin. 2006
After Finitude.
Sartre, Jean-Paul. 1943
Being and Nothingness.
Wittgenstein, Ludwig. 1953
Philosophical Investigations.
—. 1921
Tractatus Logico-Philosophicus.
Zizek, Slavoj. 2014
Event.

www.ingramcontent.com/pod-product-compliance
Lightning Source LLC
Chambersburg PA
CBHW070105070426
42448CB00038B/1725